LANDLORD TALES
AND OTHER
SHORT STORIES

Deborah J. Mansfield

authorHOUSE®

AuthorHouse™
1663 Liberty Drive
Bloomington, IN 47403
www.authorhouse.com
Phone: 1-800-839-8640

Published by AuthorHouse 4/22/2013

ISBN: 978-1-4817-4234-4 (sc)
ISBN: 978-1-4817-4233-7 (e)

Library of Congress Control Number: 2013906743

Any people depicted in stock imagery provided by Thinkstock are
models, and such images are being used for illustrative purposes only.
Certain stock imagery © Thinkstock.

This book is printed on acid-free paper.

TABLE OF CONTENTS

RUNAWAY ACTON FAIR BULLS

We were going to the Acton fair, my boys and I. It was Friday evening. It was a beautiful evening for a fair. We were just pulling into the parking area, dust was flying everywhere. We parked in the big field that led to the barn area. Everyone parked there.

My two sons, Erik and Logan were all excited, they could see all the people, animals and rides in the distance. (Logan's first fair) We were on a mission... going to Acton fair was a big thing, even though it was the smallest fair I had ever been to in my life.

I took the stroller out of the car, placed my blonde headed son in it and strapped him in. The children and I just started to walk towards the fair area from the car when movement caught the corner of my eye. Very large movement, black and white colored BIG movement. Huge bulls yoked together got loose from the owner, and were running towards the main gate. Which spills directly onto a heavily congested road, backed up with traffic, waiting in line to get into the fair.

I was three rows of cars away from the dirt road the bulls were on. They were heading our way, towards the main gate, dust pouring up behind them. Huge bulls, two of them yoked together. They were big and they were not stopping. The owner, a skinney little farmer was running behind them as fast as he could, yelling like a madman. But the bulls were too fast, they would not stop.

The gate was 100 feet from where the bulls were heading, and they were cruising. Families are walking around, cars are pulling in...I could see it all in an instant...If those bulls make it to the main gate, someone is going to get hurt or killed. Who is going to stop them?

So here I am again...In one of those situations where I have ½ a second to react. I am not lacking in the braveness quality. I've had a lot of experience in controlling large animals, grew up with horses. My sister needed some help with the horses (she was a race horse trainer, had over 100 wins at Scarborough downs), so she pointed to the barn one day and said, "help train those 3 wild stallions in the barn"...I walked in and could see they would lay their ears back and bare their teeth and try to attack people. But they didn't attack me. I felt special like a horse whisperer. I felt so special. I Love horses.

But here I was standing still, (watching the bulls get closer) all dressed up in my cute little outfit, 124 lbs. with makeup and jewelry. My reaction time of ½ a second was up. Ya ya ya...here I go again...Firmly I say to my oldest son (who behaves very well I should add) "watch your brother, I'll be right back". I didn't have time to explain as I left them in a safe place between two vehicles.

I look up to see where the bulls are now. Running fast, getting closer to the main gate.

The farmer was running behind the bulls as fast as he could, but they were too fast. I was thinking I could cut across the rows of cars and head them off. Their chain attached to their yoke was dragging 25 feet behind them. He couldn't grab the chain, couldn't reach it.

I sprint (I was second fastest in High school without trying hard) and cut across three rows of cars. I am now standing in the middle of the road now and here come

2 really big bulls heading directly towards me. 30 feet, 20 feet, 10 feet. Little old me doing this...how old was I? 30? But who else is gonna stop these beasts? BOY they are big and boy they are fast. They are getting closer and closer...I look down at my feet in the last instant. Here they are right in front of me. God they are huge. I threw my arms up in the air to make myself look larger than the 124 lbs I was, and yelled firmly "HO HO" I grabbed the chain under their chin, pulling down on the chain, yelling "HO HO", sounding commanding like a marine sergeant. Those darn things stopped. I continued to act commanding and saying "HO HO". While occasionally looking down at my feet, don't want my fancy shoes stepped on by two 3000 pound bulls.

The farmer is running up from behind. I could tell he was relieved by the look on his face as he approached. I stopped the bulls. I was proud of myself. But before he got there some strange man walked up to me while I was waiting for farmer (who was a few feet away).

It musta looked like an amusing site, here I was dressed up nice, 124 lbs., standing in the middle of the road holding 6000 lbs. of yoked together bull. So this stranger man who was walking through to the fair said "What are you doing with these bulls?" I told him I just caught them, they were running out to the main gate. The man said "you did not". Well, about this time the farmer came running up all out of breath. I handed him the chain holding his bulls. He was so grateful, he couldn't thank me enough, (in front of Mr. Stranger doubter).

After I gave him his runaway bulls. I moved along. All of this drama probably took up 45 seconds. I'm so glad I could help. I felt good about stopping those bulls. I Went and collected my kids to finish our fun evening at Acton fair. After a while we went over to the barn to look at the bulls I had stopped. There the black and white ones were yoked together, pulling thousands of pounds of cement blocks in the pulling contest. They were the biggest ones there, even won the pulling contest. Boy their evening would have been a lot different I was thinking if I wasn't in bravery mode.

BRIDGE WITH BLACK ICE

I was headed home from work on November 22. It was a cool evening. Winter was on its way. Surface ice was showing on the road, black ice, glimmering on the bridge. Cresting the hill over highway 295, heading west. The bridge I was crossing was covered with black ice. I saw a white jeep Cherokee coming in the opposite direction. Slipping and sliding, spinning around in the road, hitting the guard rail on the bridge and bouncing off. He came to a stop in the road in the middle of the bridge.

I continued in the opposite direction a little ways and pulled a "U-ey" (u turn). I had to go and make sure they were OK. The cars were stopped at the traffic lite at the bottom of the hill. They had no clue there was an accident up over the little hill crossing the bridge. They couldn't see it from where they set at the lites.

They would go right up over the hill at normal speed and at the last instant see the accident and not be able to stop on the black ice. They would have crashed and spun around like the white jeep. You cant stop on black ice. The car has a mind of its own and stops when its ready.

After turning around and heading back up the hill towards the bridge to check on the people in the white truck. I stopped in the middle of the road, got out of the car. I looked to see about 10 cars at the intersection, the light turning green and here they all come. Heading towards the accident they cannot see. They are at the bottom of the hill. They will not be able to stop when they crest the hill. They will crash into me. I am panicking...I never used my emergency flasher, didn't even know where it was. but I had to find it in ½ a second before I get crashed into. Finally I found my triangle emergency flasher button on the dash, and pushed it fast.

I jumped out of my car waving my arms frantically in the air to stop all these cars from crashing into me and into the jeep behind me. They couldn't yet see over the hill. The young couple from the jeep were standing in the middle of the road, checking out the damage to their vehicle. They didn't seem to be hurt. They were about 50 feet from where I was stopped.

And here come 10 cars coming towards me, here I am standing on black ice. Trying not to fall on my ass. I turn around and look in the opposite direction and coming from the Maine Turnpike is approx 10 more cars! I got the 10 cars on my side of the road to stop. But coming in the opposite direction the cars crested the hill, see the jeep in the middle of the road. They applied their brakes and they all went sliding all over the road. Looked like bumper cars. I couldn't believe it. Felt like It was like watching bumper cars at the fair. They were all crashing into each others vehicles (the cars had their own minds it seemed). I could see the shock on the peoples faces under the street light as they were crashing into each other. Bumper cars. Thank God the speed limit was 35 and not 50. There would have been a lot of personal injury, not just sprained wrists and necks.

People were standing in the middle of the road, in the middle of the bridge. Cars were spread all over, bumpers and fenders mangled. People could hardly walk on the road, the black ice made everything so slippery. The cars I had stopped on my side of the road had just crested the hill and they could see all the cars crash into each other, the people were standing in the middle of the road. They were grateful I stopped them.

I called the cops.

GRAMPA FROM OSLOW NORWAY

On Sunday it was a pretty regular thing to go over my grandparents for dinner.

Sitting at the dining room table next to grampa...I always liked to sit next to grampa when we went over for Sunday dinner. Sitting there waiting for grandmother to put the food on the table. Lets get it done gram...which let me remind you was the best cookin in the world. I miss my grandmother, she was my gods angel sent to earth. She loved me, talked to me, fed me and gave me candy. What more could a kid ask for?

Sitting around the old dining room table, as dinner progressed...here comes the stories...by grampa from Oslow, Norway. One in particular I remember...

It was 1914, World War I was going on. Carl was the oldest of 12 children, living in the hills of Oslow Norway. 12 years old and bored to death. He heard of the promises of the New World in America. So at 6 feet tall a young Viking man set sail with his friend Lars to see for themselves what America was like. What it had to offer. Set sail on a clipper ship bound for America.

It was cold, bone chilling cold, so cold my teeth chattered, said grampa with his beer in hand. He always had his beer with dinner. His job was to be a look out in the crows nest of the old clipper ship. He would have to climb up the tallest mast to the little crows nest and keep a look out for other boats and land. He thought he was going to freeze to death up there in the crows nest. He was never so cold in all his life. Grandmothers eyes were glued to grampa as he told his story. You could tell she really felt his story. Maybe it was because her oldest brother froze in the trenches in France during World War I. This was about the same time.

He made the decision to go below and try to get warm for a while.

Grampa could hardly move his fingers to crawl down from the crows nest onto the mast. He almost fell trying to climb down the ropes. He had to get warm and get some food. While on deck he heard the men yelling for him. It was not just a friendly yell either. They were looking for him to throw him overboard for leaving his post at the nest. They were yelling Carl, Carl...almost sounded like a crow said grampa. While he ran and hid below near the storage crates, in the bowels of the boat...listening to them call for him. What was he going to do? Go out to them when they called him...to get thrown overboard. That's what they do. He had to hide on the boat for a week until they landed in America. His friend Lars brought him food to his hiding place. That was dark and cold too, but not as cold as the crows nest with the wind and freezing spray.

When we docked in America I waited till the coast was clear and snuck off the boat in Boston, Massachusetts. I've never seen my family since I left Oslow Norway in 1914, since I was 12 years old. But I saw a newspaper article 40 years later that mentioned 5 kids with the same last name as I, born on the same day in Oslow, Norway. Sounds like a Viking story. Too, years later a man named Lars came to my front door in Sudbury, Mass. looking for me. I wasn't home. Grammy answered the door and said I wasn't home. He never came back. I waited for him to come back.

I loved those dinner stories by grampa. Ethel told a fish story that day too. They went fishing and harpooned a big fish in the Bay of Maine. Had a long rope attached to the harpoon with a barrel tied to the end she said. After the fish was harpooned it came up along side the 18 foot boat and she stood up to take a picture of it and its head went past one end of the boat and its tail was past the other. She looked in a book after and come to find out it was a great white shark. Nice fish story.

It was enjoyable to have dinner at grammy and grampas many years ago.

GUN ON MATT

I happened to be driving through town on my way home from work. I saw my best friend Matt in his truck and pulled up next to him to chat for a few. Small talk. Well, he was all proud, he fixed his transmission in his truck all by himself. He pulled away from me in his vehicle with a little "chirp" of the tires. That's a guy thing, showing off with a little peel out and a chirp of the tires.

Well, what happened next, I had to write a short letter to the Chief of Sandore, Maine police department and cc the State Police and Governor. I guess what really freaked me out about this police traffic stop was that in another county a few days earlier, a cop shot and killed a young man who pulled out his cell phone and the cop thought it was a gun. And this cop had that attitude like he was going to shoot my friend.

Here is my letter...

Dear Sir...

On 7-6-01 at approx 10:30 p.m. my friend Matt Michael was stopped by Sandore Police for minor tire noise. I saw the whole thing. I drove by the traffic stop and pulled into the parking lot behind the bank, approx 50 feet from Matt's vehicle. I leaned on the fender of my car to watch and asked Matt if he was ok and what was going on. Well, next thing I know Officer Captain gets out of the cruiser fast and yells at me to "get away, I am interfering with an investigation, and to go" Well, I go to walk away and I tell officer Captain to "be nice". I get over by my car and I turn back to look, and Officer Captain had his weapon drawn. He was approximately ten feet behind Matts vehicle. Had his gun aimed at Matt's head. Yelling "put your hands in the air Matt!" I couldn't believe Officer Captain was acting like that for no reason. Matt didn't do anything except chirp his tires a little. He doesn't own a gun or carry one. He is retired special forces green beret, and deserves the respect by the police. He protects the innocent and has lived in this town for years.

Well anyway...I jumped into my car and called Sandore Police Department and said "one of your boys is holding a gun on my friend at the top of Washington Street. If you don't give me someone to handle this I will call the State Police to handle this". I was put on hold and then hung up after a little while. I could hear the crackle of Officer Captains radio as he went to answer it. I looked over and Officer Captain put his gun away and got in his cruiser "Have a good night Mr. Michael", and he drove away. Then Matt drove off.

Excuse me, but we should have more respect for our Vets. Our town is safer with them in it. It was very scary watching Officer Captain hold a gun on my friend. I don't appreciate it.

Sincerely, Deborah

So I found Matt down the street and asked him what in hell that was all about. He said that's the second time that cop pulled a gun on him. When they were in Desert Storm that cop was a peon, and Matt was special, he's always been jealous, now he's got more power.

Whatever...I said, as long as you are ok.

I GOT ROBBED

I drove into my driveway. Just got home from work. Pulling in, I was driving around the back of my house to park on the side by the porch. I noticed my bedroom light on. I never leave my bedroom light in. And then, I saw my back door wide open, which is always locked.

I freaked. I pulled into my parking spot as fast as I could. Jumped out of my car and ran up to the front door (which was locked). They didn't get in through this way I thought.

I called the cops, they got on the line right away. Keeping them on the phone while entering my home, the girl on dispatch said "don't go in, wait for the police". I was going in. I was bullshit. I lived here ten years and never got broken into. I was gonna kill the guy.

I was nervous and scared. I kept looking around the kitchen for someone in my home. I was really mad and growling, "who the fuck broke into my home, I'm gonna kill you!" I thought they were hiding somewhere or ran out the back door. My kitchen door that went out towards the back door was broken off it's hinges.

My poor bird. I have a beautiful green congor parrot who does not like noise or new people. He's a hermit. He must have been screeching and screaming. He bickers when he's disturbed. Even when I talk on the phone or if the TV. is going, he bitches. My sister gave me that bird cause he used to bitch so much. Now, when I write this story, to have peace and quiet, and not be bitched at, I have to put my bird Java in a cage and put him in another room. His screeching gives me a headache. Go to your room Java.

I'm surprised the neighbors upstairs didn't hear my bird crab. Java is so loud. When they broke in through the back kitchen door, they used a hammer to tear the door off it's hinge. I found the hammer the next morning by the back door on the ground.

It is interesting to note that I did call the Sandore, Maine police about a week before this. I felt like I was going to be broken into. I talked to Officer Carot and asked who would be a good alarm company to get. Who would he recommend? He said he can't advise me. I told him I felt like I was going to be broken into. He said there is nothing he can do. So much for the cops.

Well, less than a week later I was broken into and robbed. Here I was, standing in the middle of my kitchen, after being robbed, waiting for the police. I felt like I had been raped ten times over. My home is my sacred place. I kept looking around for missing items, while waiting for the police. I couldn't find anyone in the house.

A blue eyed cop pulled up. Handsome, I thought. He said, "don't go in the house yet". I already did. He went in and saw my broken door. We walked around the back of my home and found a broken cellar window. That was where the guy entered.

Within myself, I knew who broke in. But no one saw him do it. I rented out the upstairs apartment to a young woman with two children. Sometimes her boyfriend would come over. He was the local heroin, drug addict. I felt very strongly that her boyfriend Ray was the one who broke into my house. This was that same strong feeling I had when I felt like I was going to be broken into. Did the girl upstairs hear anything? I ran upstairs and saw Melissa in her kitchen and asked if she heard anything. I got broken into I told her. She said she was home all day and didn't hear anything. She didn't hear the kitchen door being torn off it's hinges by a hammer? She didn't hear my bird screaming for his life? And you were home all day, I said sarcastically. "You didn't hear anything?, and your boyfriend Ray didn't either?" She said she hadn't seen him all day.

I walked out of her apartment and down the stairs. There sitting on her front porch was Ray. "What's wrong?" he said. I growled "You piece of shit, broke into my apartment!" Of course he denied it. I was very growley with him, but not violent. It was all in my voice. I was bullshit. My mouth went on and on. I knew in my heart it was him.

The blue eyed cop thought me and Ray were going to get into a fight. Ray used to be a golden gloves boxer and I was a fifty two year old female. So the cop told me to shut up and get in the house. Ya, I went into my house and I turned around to the cops face I said, "That guy robbed me and you are telling me to shut up?! If he robbed your house, you would kill him!" This is my home. I've lived here along time and never got broken into. Now the biggest heroin addict, drug addict in the area has been hanging around for a few months, and all the houses in my neighborhood are getting broken into. But he said he didn't do it. Even though he has a reputation for robbing disabled people, people in wheel chairs, and waiting in the dark by peoples doors around social security check time. Jumping and robbing citizens for money and prescription drugs. Blue eyes said he didn't need another incident. He knew Ray liked to beat up innocent people and rob them. I was very perturbed. The cop was just doing his job. He didn't want to write out another police report. He gave me a police report to fill out and make a list of what was missing. the cop said, "they usually look for drugs or money, and jewelry to pawn." I walked through my home. It didn't feel like home anymore. I called my son Logan to tell him I got broken into. Could he come and secure my back door and window for me? At 12 o'clock at night. He was bullshit. He knew it was Ray that broke in. If Ray was out front when my son pulled in, he would have pounded him into the ground. Golden gloves or not.

I was looking around for missing items. My daughter's little diamond ring she wore as a young girl, and my father's Masonic ring he wore for fifty years of his life was gone. That ring was the only thing I wanted from my step father when he died. Those items were special. Other jewelry was missing and a bunch of change. I didn't notice until later that a few of my beautiful shirts were missing. I found a small bowl that had change missing out of it, he had dumped out. I called the cops the next day and asked them to fingerprint test it.

The cops came over and put the bowl in a plastic bag. A

few days later I called to find out who's prints were on it. Too, they dusted for prints around my cellar window. No match they said, on either. Those were pretty fresh prints. I could see them clearly on the white cellar window (which was installed ten years ago) standing out in the black fingerprint dust. But the cops said there wasn't a match, he probably wore gloves. I didn't believe them.

Well. I know a few people around town and on the street. I started asking a few questions about Ray, the thief, the drug addict. Come to find out, Ray went around town bragging to people and my friend Lisa's son. He bragged that was him that robbed me and the cops couldn't do anything about it. he said he was gonna jump me some night when I got home from work.

I went to some of my close neighbors homes to tell them I got robbed and to do a community crime watch. I was respected by my neighbors and we were all going to work together to make the neighborhood safer. I used to be a security cop. My neighbors across the street told me a lot about the history of Ray's thieving. Even his own father said someone is going to kill him someday. They caught him head stomping his girlfriend on the sidewalk last week and the cops let him go. Why?

I have an invisible black cape and am known for

protecting the innocent. But this really upset me. I usually help others. Now I needed help.

Approximately one month later, after Ray had robbed a few more people around town. He was walking down Island Avenue about seven a.m. with his girlfriend. Guess who's path he crossed? Bobs. We love Bob. Well, Ray said to Bob "Hey, I feel like fighting." Bob (local really tough guy) knew about Ray robbing everyone around town and the cops never did anything about it. So Bob said, "sure Ray, let's fight." Bob can bench press 500 pounds. Time to kick Rays ass! He deserves it! I would love to be a fly on the wall and watch this fight. If you could call it that.

After Ray threw a punch, Bob picked him up and slammed him down on the ground. "You like to rob old ladies Ray?!" He slammed him down on the ground again. (Ray was only 160 pounds) "You like to jump and rob disabled people Ray?!" SLAM, SLAM, SLAM...Ray curled up in a fetal position on the ground and covered his head with his hands. Bob jumped on him, pounding his ribs and head. "You like to beat up defenseless people and women Ray?!" "You want to fight?' "Get up and fight you pussy!" Ray's girlfriend started yelling "stop Bob, you are going to kill him!" Bob slammed him down on the ground one last time for good measure. "I better not hear about you robbing anyone else Ray or you are going to get another beating.

A crowd was gathering and people were looking out their windows. Everyone on the street knew Ray and knew what he does to innocent people. Everyone was happy about Ray getting beat. Bob walked away. Mission accomplished. You wonder if Bob had this planned. He did have a reputation for protecting the innocent.

Well, Bob walked away, went around the corner, and here comes a Sandore cop. "You here for me?" Bob asks the cop. "No, why?" asks the cop. I just kicked Ray Bodins ass. The cop said good and walked away. I gave Bob $100 for his broken finger trouble, doctor bills. Ray ended up with three broken ribs.

It still bothered me why the cops didn't do anything and I wanted to know why. I put the word out on the street. Was Ray an informant? Is that why he could rob people, attack them and beat up women? The cops can't say he's an informant. I called an agent and he told me that.

A few weeks later someone dropped me off a paper to read. It was a paper from the Maine DEA (drug enforcement agency) with Rays name on it and date of birth (how ironic he robbed me on his birthday). There was even his signature and three DEA agents names and signatures on it. He was being used by the DEA to buy drugs. Thats why they let him rob and beat up people. He always got away with it. They have been creating a monster. When he bought drugs for the DEA he would take some out before he gave it to them. Our tax dollars at work. I lived in my home for ten years and never got broken into. And now the cops cover it up. Protecting the innocent. I have an alarm system now.

LANDLORD ON ELM STREET STORIES

SHE LIVED

One day I took a break from work (being a landlord) needing a cup of tea, snack and a girls room. I went inside my office. I heard an urgent knock on the front door. There it was again...knock, knock, knock. I opened the door quickly, not knowing what to expect. I'm faced with a ten year old boy who lived with his mother upstairs in one of the apartments I rented out. Well, he was very upset.... "Landlordlady (that's what the kids in the neighborhood renamed me) come quick...my mom wont wake up, I keep trying to wake her up and she wont wake up." "She always told me to come and get you if something is wrong, and I think something's wrong with my mom." There was such an urgency in his voice. He was lucky to catch me, I would not have been there in a few minutes.

I put my cup of tea down and followed him out the door and up the stairs. He was running. I followed him into the apartment. As I was entering I could see his moms legs on the living room floor. Going into the living room, I could see Mandy was unconscious on the floor, face up, her head cocked sideways against the stool. I didn't know if she had fallen or what. This all happened so fast. Her face was pale, she looked like she was dead. Too pretty to be dead I thought. Her son was crying by my side "my mom, my mom".

I pulled her by her two feet to straighten out her neck. Her breathing seemed restricted because of the position of her head and neck. I fell to my knees at her side and called 911. 911: I need an ambulance fast, shes unconscious, not breathing, we need help ASAP. Not two minutes passed and a skinny Biddefrog cop walked in the door with his flashlite.

Mandy's son Dean was at my side crying. I kept my arm around his shoulders and comforted him as we waited for the ambulance. We stood over her as she lay face up, motionless. The cop shined the flashlight in her eyes, her pupils did not dilate at all, usually that means brain death. The reason why I know that is because my husband died brain death from motorcycle injury. I looked at the cop, we shook our heads. We didn't want to upset her son. Without saying we knew she was probably dead. Not a good sign when the pupils fail to dilate.

The cop said "Go tell the ambulance to bring the stretcher up right away, don't waste any time". We had to be careful of not alarming the son more than what he already was. He was crying at my side.

I had to run out to the deck to yell to the ambulance attendants below to bring the stretcher right away. Thank God they did. If things did not move along as fast as they did, as far as getting Mandy oxygen and proper care, the outcome would have been different and not good.

It was awkward carrying her on the stretcher out the narrow hallway. The ambulance attendants took her, red lights and siren blaring. I kept the boy till the dad came to get him. He was traumatized. The Biddefrog cop went on his way.

I stopped by the hospital the next day to see Mandy, see how she was. I expected to see her in a coma or dead. There she was sitting up in a chair, out of it. She was alive. I couldn't believe it. I thought she was dead last night. Every time I see her now I feel like I'm seeing a resurrected person, and I have to hug her. She said she would be dead if things didn't happen so fast as far as saving her life. Made me happy. Her son has his mom. She is still my tenant and her life is better now. Next time she has a headache she wont take pills from strangers.

SACO RIVER STORY

At first I didn't take much interest in the story Grandmother told about Chief Sitting Bull and the Saco River. Until I started to notice strange occurrences happening.

Ruth is the great granddaughter of Chief Sitting Bull. She would sit in the doorway of her apartment building, in her wheelchair. Smoking her cigarettes, watching people go by. She was a quiet old woman, but when she spoke, people listened. Her room was covered wall to floor with Indian pictures and feathers. I felt like I was walking into a teepee when I entered her room.

Sometimes I would have to walk in and out of her doorway where she was sitting. Over the years I have gotten to know her better. Sometimes I would sit with her there on the front step and have Indian tea, and we would talk.

I have heard about the story of the curse on the Saco River by Chief Sitting Bull. People talk. But I never heard it from a descendant of Chief Sitting Bull. I felt fortunate that Grandmother (as we all call her now) would tell me the story of her great-grandfather Chief Sitting Bull.

The front granite steps was cool on my ass, as I set there listening to Grandmother tell the story. Her grandchildren playing at her our feet. The boys remind me of young Indian boys, who should be riding pinto ponies across the prairies, hooping and hollering. They looked like Indians. I went to a Pow-Wow (Indian gathering) with them last summer. They looked more like Indians than anyone else there.

Grandmother wanted to tell me the story, and I wanted to hear it. I've been waiting quite a while to hear this. Her brow lowered. She leaned over towards me and got a stern look on her face. "Those bastards", she said...Many years ago Chief Sitting Bull, my great grandfather, lived by the Saco River. One day some white men came along. They captured and restrained Sitting Bull. They took his wife and year old baby. They slit the wife's throat and threw her in the Saco River. They threw the baby boy in the Saco River too. There was a strong current. They both died. Sitting Bull was beside himself with grief and anguish. In his anger and hurt, he cursed the Saco River. He said, "someone would die in the Saco River every year". People had gathered from the neighborhood to hear Grandmothers story. The granite step was covered with people. It was interesting hearing this story from Grandmother.

A few months pass...

In April, a creepy guy tried to grab and abduct the great-great granddaughter of Chief Sitting Bull. He grabbed her by the arm and was trying to pull her away from her mother. This happened just two houses up the street from her home. The mom Tammy was pulling on her daughters arm and thought she was going to pull her daughters arm off. The man was pulling on her so hard. She didn't even know this man and here he was trying to pull her daughter away from her. Tammy was screaming for help. Someone driving by in a car stopped and jumped out to help. The creepy abductor let go of the girls arm when he saw people coming to help. He ran down between some buildings outback. Tammy called me, she called the cops too. The man was gone.

Everyone who had gathered around was looking for the

creepy guy who tried to steal Mariah. He ran off. No one could find him. The police took a report. The rookie cops told us later that if this had happened in Biddefrog Pool, they'd be all over it. But because this happened in a poor neighborhood, they weren't interested in pursuing an investigation. Didn't that get my goat when I heard that. So, knowing the family, I went into conference with the mom Tammy. We were going to capture the guy and keep and eye out.

I told Tammy I was an artist and I will come over and get a description of him. She can tell me what he looks like and I will draw him. Like a police sketch artist. Portraits are so boring for me to draw, but I knew I could draw it. I'd do whatever it took to protect the kids in the neighborhood.

We sat down at Tammy's kitchen table. Grandmother and the kids were in the living room. Everyone was perturbed about this attempted abduction.

I had my pencil in hand, ready to draw. I said to Tammy, "you need to describe in detail as much as you can remember of him. By the time I am done drawing his face, if it looks like him, you will be upset. We went over as much as we could. Glasses, face, hair, jacket description, etc.. After forty five minutes his face was done. She got real quiet and started to cry. She had to get up from the table and leave the room. She went into the living room and hugged her daughter for quite a while, and kissed her on her forehead. Grandmother sat still and quiet. She watched. Three generations of descendants of Chief Sitting Bull in one room. I was honored to know these Indians.

Well, the portrait was finished. I took it to the local police. Gave them a copy.

Tammy said to me, "next time I see that guy I will call you first before I call the cops".

"Ok", I said, "lets do it Tammy".

One week later, Tammy calls me, freaking out. "He just walked by my house and went up the street, but he didn't go by the house on the corner!" He must have gone inside. There was an urgency in her voice. "OK", I said. I ran up the street. looking at the building, I was trying to figure which apartment he went into. I chose right. The first one I went to...I knocked and asked if a man in a brown leather jacket with glasses was in their apartment. here he comes walking out of the back room straight at me. Just as Tammy described him, and as I drew. I was in shock. He walked towards me. I was so nervous, but I had to do this. Bastard, try to take one of our kids off of Elm Street, I thought.

There he was right in my face, wondering what I wanted. I said to him, "you need to be identified by the police, you tried to take a kid off of Elm Street last week". He got closer to my face. I was creeped out. I thought he was gonna hit me. "Are you crazy?!", he says, and starts belittling me and putting me down. Which all that didn't work with me, he still needed to be identified.

While he is in my face, calling me names, I called the cops. He was saying he was a master mason, and he didn't try to take a kid. I said, "I didn't care what mens club he belonged to" (though my father was a mason and I have the highest respect for good masons) He needed to be identified. He needed to be talked to by the police.

I was on the phone with the cops, dispatch wanted a description of him in case he ran off. That I gave, while he was getting in my face insulting me. I had to keep backing intimidate me.

One cop showed up. He took the guys identification. I called Tammy, the mom, who was waiting down the street with her daughter and a bunch of people. The cop, who had creepy guy detained up the street, wanted Tammy and Mariah to see his face. He wanted to make sure they had the right guy. Mariah was so scared, but she was so brave. She walked up the sidewalk towards the cop and the creepy guy (to identify him). Mariah had two tough guys (local boys) on each side of her for support. When she saw the creepy guy walking down the sidewalk towards her, she turned around, screamed and ran. "It's him! it's him!" she screamed and ran into her mothers arms down the street.

Tammy was very upset. She was a very strong woman at 300 pounds, she could kick anyone's ass. But she was shaking like a leaf in the wind. She peeked around the corner of the building and said it was him. Everyone in the neighborhood had gathered around and was watching. There are a lot of people who live on Elm Street.

The cop walked back up the street with the guy. He told him to stay away from this street and let him go. We couldn't believe it, he let him go.

Grandmother says "You don't fuck with the Great Spirit". It was so funny to see a little old lady in a wheelchair say that. But she seems so powerful in her quietness.

I met these people when their house was burning down in the middle of a freezing winter. It was an eight alarm fire right down the street from my building. Everyone in the neighborhood was walking down to watch. I walked down there too and I see a little old lady in a wheelchair.

She was in the middle of the sidewalk, with five blankets in her lap and a dog in her lap. She was freezing. Her house was burning down behind her. It was so sad. Her daughter was standing in the street, in stocking feet. It was 10 below zero. She was crying. I walked up to her and said I was sorry. Someone introduced us. She said she lost everything and was homeless. Her house was burning down as she spoke. She had a blanket over her shoulders and was shivering.

I had my fingers on a key in my pocket. That key was to a four bedroom apartment that just went empty up the street. I was turning the key over and over in my hand as I pulled it out of my pocket. I was watching. I saw Grandmother shivering in her wheelchair. The ice was building up on everything from the fire hoses shooting water everywhere to keep other buildings from catching fire. Tammy was freezing in her stocking feet. She said she was homeless with her 3 kids, mom, and boyfriend. I faced her and said, "no your not" and I gave her the key to an apartment just up the street. She started crying even more. "Are you serious?", she said. Yes, I replied You can go there tonight. It's heated. It just seemed like the right thing to do. These people lived in that apartment for about three years after the fire.

Well, the cops never did anything about the creepy

attempted abductor guy. And of course he tried to turn everything around to blame it on the child or me.

Well...Shit happened...

As Grandmother said, "You don't fuck with the Great Spirit". Or chief Sitting Bulls descendants. Usually about one person dies in the Saco River a year. Within 3 months six people died in the Saco River, shortly after this attempted abduction. There has never been so many people die in the Saco River in one summer. A twelve year old kid drowned. he fell off the wall into the water. The fire department fished out a fifty year old man who was in the water for a couple weeks. Too, a drunk man and his girlfriend were fighting. They were driving in his van and took a corner too fast and landed in the Saco River. And there were two more victims. I don't know how they met their demise in the Saco River.

During this summer. After the attempted abduction of Sitting Bulls great great granddaughter. The attempted abductors (creepy guy) dad died. His sister was shot and killed by the police. He tried to hang himself shortly after. And the head detective who shut down on the attempted abduction case was stabbed in the hand at the police department by a criminal. Weird occurrences. As Grandmother says.

I wrote a song dedicated to these people:

SACO RIVER SONG

Saco River...Its a powerful river...Its a strong river...Grandmother says........................

Listen to the Great Spirit...As the water rolls...Down to the ocean...Grandmother says......................

LOCAL GUYS AND THEIR STUPID GANG WARS

It was about 10 p.m. on a Friday night. I was walking across the back yard behind my building to go check on a motion sensor lite.

There in the middle of the back yard was a circle of about 15 to 20 young men, aged 20 to 30 years old. They had chains, bats and pipes in their hands ready to go have a gang war, or to kick someone's ass, I thought.

I didn't know that when you bought buildings on Elm Street that it needed so much drama control over there. There was a gang war or fight up under the street lights on the corner last weekend and two young men ended up in the emergency room.

Well, me being mother hen (and renamed Landlord

Lady by the kids on the street), not wanting un-necessary fighting on my side of the street. I proceeded to walk in the middle of this circle of young men and say "looks like we are going to have a gang war...not on my side of the street!" Brandon said, "We are going to take it up under the streetlights, on the corner like last weekend. And do you think you are our mother?" "Yes, I do I replied, the police are already on their way."

They all dispersed, it didn't take them too long knowing the police were on the way. Wing nuts. But they respected me because they know I am good and fair to the people on the street so I didn't get beat.

Too, a couple years prior to this incident 15 young men went to another tenants apartment to kick someone's ass cause he choked out his girlfriend. It was her old boyfriend who was going to kick Chris's ass with 14 helpers.

Well who does Chris call but another tenant Logan who lives up the street in another apartment. "Logan, come quick there are 15 guys outside my front door and they want to beat me up." Well, Logan was respected in the community. He comes walking down. The guys were yelling at each other. But it was not a fair fight 15 to 1. So Logan says, "ok, you want to kick his ass for choking out his girlfriend?" Logan doesn't believe in beating women.

Logan made them both empty their pockets of keys and sharp objects. Making it a fair fight, one on one, and no sharp objects to hurt anyone. By then about 50 people had gathered out back. Logan said to make a circle around the 2 men, letting it be a fair fight. my other tenant Leslie was watching her favorite show on TV. and said this was more interesting than her favorite soap opera. So she put her chair in front of the window that faced out back and pulled the curtains apart to watch the fight.

Chris got his ass kicked by Tom in less than a minute. He said he deserved it for choking out a girl. He went to walk away and Tom went to attack him. Logan said, "thats enough he learned his lesson."

I've noticed that in this town there seems to be beating sessions at parties. But there isn't as many as before.

GETTING STARTED IN REALESTATE

I bought my first home (a trailer in a trailer park) when I was about 30 years old. It was so exciting getting my first place with my two children in a park where there was alot of kids for them to play with. Though it was a trailer, it was home, and it was beautiful to us. I had my own apartment since I was 15 years old and wanted something in my name. My mother worked in real estate. I would stop into her office and watch and listen. I would skim through the Multiple Listing Service book just to check things out. I learned a lot just by seeing and watching. My mom always advised me to keep things in my name if I ever bought a place. Now I see the wisdom in that. I'm the only one who controls my properties.

The year was about 1985. I found a trailer in a trailer park with big bow windows in the front. I paid about $19,000 for it. I owned it for one and a half years. I bought it through an FHA first time home buyers loan at low interest. My mom lent me the $3000. down payment to buy the place. I loved it and the children loved it more.

Well, I ended up pregnant and engaged. My fiancé wanted me close to his family, this was his first child and his parents first grandchild. My boyfriend gave me two acres of land in my name and I bought a new trailer and put it on the land. So we moved into my new trailer. This was 1987. My daughter was born three months later.

Then my first trailer sold for almost $27,000. I couldn't believe it. I was going to have almost $10,000. in my hand. I called the bank and told them I need to cash a check for this and wanted hundreds. I wanted to look at all that money for a while and think about how this money could make more money in the future. I didn't just want to spend it on junk. I have never seen so much money in my hands, in my life. I went into the bank to cash my check. My friend Danny the cop was with me for security reasons. He was standing behind me. The teller mentioned to me that I should be careful carrying all this money around. And Danny opened his jacket revealing his gun and he said , "that's ok, shes with me". The teller was paranoid seeing the gun.. I told her he was a cop. He came with me. It was kinda funny. You shoulda seen the look on her face.

At this period of time, real estate prices were rising and it was a good time to sell. In looking for a property, I found one a mile and a half down the road from where I lived. Perfect. it was a tiny little house on a third acre for $39,000.00, this was 1988. It needed a lot of work. I bought it, fixed it up and rented it out. Do you know I did all this on my income? I received about $13,00.00 a month Social Security benefits as a widow and did this. I was proud of myself.

After fifteen years the loans are almost paid off. So I saved my money and used the equity in a property to buy a 2 unit. (Which I live in now for over ten years). Then I used the equity from the second trailer ($69,000.00) to buy an eight unit for $275,000.00.

Fast forward to 2011. Now I have 9 buildings. I have learned alot running buildings. This is my job. It is a soap opera too. This is why I am compelled to write Landlord Stories by Landlord Lady (renamed by all the local kids). All these different situations that cross my path should be told. I am thankful to God (or the Great

Spirit) for all the people that have crossed my path in this line of work.

I received Social Security for myself and my son. As a widow I received benefits (my husband died in a motorcycle accident). I had to pay rent somewhere, so I thought...why not own? Over the years I gained equity in my little junky places. Always when I got money I put it back into the business. Larry helped me to get where I am today in my business. Thank God for Larry. I used that equity (at a time when the economy was good) Larry lent me money and helped me. Now I run buildings full time, I've quit my other job. It has been like taking a thousand college courses running buildings. I do my own evictions now, drama control coordinator and fixaholic. Ive become a fixaholic.. You've heard of drug addicts and alcoholics...well, I'm a fixaholic. I have taught myself how to run buildings. But I wouldn't change what I have learned from my experience and interactions with people as Landlord Lady.

For years I have wanted to write a book. All the situations that cross my path I feel I should share. So Landlord Stories are coming first. I am thankful to God for all the cool people I have met being a landlord. Some people I don't like. I'm not trying to fool you there. I have a strong personality and am not afraid to use it. I usto train wild race horses and people are a lot smaller than them.

I bought old buildings that the last landlords didn't take care of very well. I used all my equity to repair, bring up to codes, keep heated, and safe for the people. I've had over twenty families move back into my buildings (that had previously moved out) because I care about the people. It's not just a job. I'm like mother hen. I used to be a security cop. Done a lot of different things through the years. But we need community today. Wherever we are we need to make the children feel safe and protect the innocent. If people are being idiots my tenants usually call me first before the cops. I get over there and crab at them like their mom would. I tell them if you can't get along in the main living area to shut up and go to your room. Don't even talk to each other. If I have to come back, I'll have the cops behind me. They usually are good, or it's quieter for a while. The cops come with power trip with patches, paid for by the people, to throw tickets around. The people cannot afford that.

Where some of the buildings are in close proximity to each other, in the summer we have big cookouts. I buy a lot of food and popsicles. We block off the back yard and driveway. We let all the little kids play, run around, and ride bikes. Reminds me of Cat Stevens song "where do the children play?". While the children play, Wilber cooks. He used to be a fancy cook at a fancy restaurant. We got Wilber to cook for us now, na na. All the children love Wilber.

There are a variety of people who live in my apartments. Some have very colorful pasts (which all those stories would be short stories within themselves). But what is especially nice about some of these people is that they respect the community that we've established. They keep the pedophiles out, drug addicts, and protect the children. Sometimes strong personalities come in handy if they are on your side. If you respect people and are fair to them, it means the world to them, because their lives and families have been really screwed up. They greatly appreciate people who are honest, fair, and straight with them. I want those people on my side. Protecting the community. Though sometimes they can be stupid bastards .

Now I am running buildings in the middle of a depression. The government says we aren't in a depression. I must disagree. In a two year span I've had 30 apartments go empty out of 31. I've never seen so many families lose jobs, homes, and not have food. This is in the United States of America. Families are doubling up. Older children are moving in with parents.

They cannot afford their own places anymore. I think this is what people have to do to survive.

My water and sewer bills are high because people need to share living spaces. They would be homeless. The homeless shelters are full. What do I do? Throw out 35 people from my apartments? Who are doubling up with their friends and family in order to have a roof over their heads and survive. I cannot do that. I wrote a grant proposal to try to save my buildings and all the people dependant on me running them. But I couldn't find a funder for my grant proposal.

Our government gives billions of our tax dollars to banks to save the banks. These banks turn around after being given billions, and shut down and foreclose on thousands of peoples homes and apartments. The home owners have paid billions of dollars of profit interest to these banks for years. Now the homeowner or landlord is behind on payments. The banks say...pay all past due or get out. Throw thousands of families out of their homes and businesses during a depression. I wrote a letter to my banks because I am trying to keep my business running, keep people in their places and from homelessness.

This is my 3 page letter I wrote to the bank:

Dear Bank...

My plan is to work on keeping my building. To keep up on taxes, insurance and repairs. Keep up to codes and rented. I love my building even though old and junky. Oil is too expensive. The economy is horrid. We are in a depression. Oil is so expensive alot of landlords ran out this winter. Maine is very cold in wintertime. Alot of people don't want to invest in real estate where oil costs so much. People are having trouble finding jobs.

A lot of properties are for sale in the southern Maine area, and they are not selling. Families are walking away from their homes and sharing space with friends and family in order to survive. Landlords are walking away from buildings because they are too expensive to run. February 2011 was the worst month for home sales in the U.S.A. for 50 years.

A lot of banks that have foreclosed are stuck with buildings they cannot sell. The banks must heat and maintain, and prevent break-ins. I have noticed it is best for banks to work with owners to keep building inhabited and running. Keep people in them so they don't get broken into. They are breaking in all over. Too, there is an infestation of bed bugs across the U.S.A. and it costs a lot to get rid of them. I have that problem off and on.

I am doing my best to "crawl up out of the hole" financially. This is an old building. If the roof leaks, furnace needs work, plumbing and electrical too. It must be taken care of to keep the building safe and up to codes. If I let things go and don't heat my building, I cannot keep rented. Codes will shut down. They are doing that.

What will the banks do when oil goes to $4.00 + $5.00 a gallon? We will not be able to afford to heat our homes in Maine, in the winter. The banks might have to let borrowers not pay payments for the worst 3-4 months of the winter. The choice would be to shut down building cause no-one can afford to heat it and let the bank forclose in a market area where people cannot afford to heat a building in the winter. Never mind make payments.

I should think a bank would be proud to have someone stick by their building through the worst depression in history. Empty houses are being stripped for copper and saleable materials. We are all screwed financially because of the economy. We are all on the same boat. Please don't take my building. I don't mean to sound like a crybaby, but this is my job too. Please throw me a life-line, but one that will not break. Do not make my payments so high monthly that I cannot even pay for bills, repairs, taxes, insurance, and oil. Please help. Our government gave the banks billions of dollars to be saved. I want to be saved too.

I would like to put my past due amount on the end of my loan (forbearance) and to modify my loan. This is my job.

Thank you, Me

Maybe Steven King didn't need the money for his stories as bad as I do. (We love Steven and Tabitha) But I have a lot of families dependant on me being Landlord Lady. Yes, I need to sell at least 100,000 copies of Landlord Stories. I would love to create new jobs, new business, open a food pantry for the poor and go down on my tenants rent.

It makes me sad when I go into a tenants house and open the refrigerator and see no milk for the little kids in the apartment. Or they are sick and need medicine. To me this is a sin. I give them $ for milk, medicine or supper to hold them over. Not much $ cause I'm poor too, only with more zeros on the end of my bills. How do we ignore people in need? Especially children who are innocent in this crazy world, they only need milk and supper. I cannot. I got into being a landlord as a job, but because of the depression I've never seen so much hardship. God sees everything. We must help the poor. But in the meantime we are all screwed financially. I'm worst off with more zeros on the end of my bills.

A lot of people have crossed my path in my life. I hope their lives are better from me being their Landlord Lady. I have even saved some lives.

TIPPING OVER OLAF

It was wintertime. It snowed about a foot and a half. Which is not unusual for Maine in the winter. I was out in my Dodge 4x4 plow truck. It was part of my Landlord job and I loved to plow. I was out all day plowing different driveways. The air was crisp and clear, I was tired and wanted a hot chocolate before I headed home. Seeing the lights in the distance of a local "eatery, bar, pool hall" I pulled in. Walking in, shaking off the snow. I see Olaf sitting at the corner of the bar. Crazy Norseman he is, but he's my friend. I headed over towards him and set down right next to him. He is a big boy. About 350 pounds. Only one guy in town could beat up Olaf and he wasn't there. I felt like a little bird next to a grizzly bear, and I was a female. I wasn't afraid of him, because he respected me. But if you rub his fur the wrong way, you better back up. Last week he threw a guy through the wall. So now he was on probation in that place. One more incident and he was out. You wonder if some of the injections they give to some of these men in the Gulf war makes them crazier than normal. Or maybe he's got psychological issues stemming back to his childhood (like all of us). But the man has a heart of gold for being a crazy bastard. But tonight he was drunk.

One day about three years ago, I was waitressing at the end of Old Orchard Beach pier. Olaf was the bouncer, the biggest one there. The bikini contest was getting ready to start. The place was packed with drunk young men, waiting to see the girls. Let me add, this was not a strip club. A lot of people came from out of the country, and from out of state. Even gangs like the Bloods and Crips, to enjoy the beach area. The majority of the population was white. But there was a gang of about 25 blacks from New York City at the end of the pier. This group had already been warned by the bouncers (a few times). They were drinking shots of tequila by the gallons. Seemed like they were playing the reverse racism card. They were very disrespectful. One of these guys pulled the string on a white girls bikini (when she was walking by) and her top almost fell off. Her husband stood up to fight with the string puller. All hell broke loose. I was waiting on a table and stopped. The men started yelling "throw them off the Pier!" It was deafening 300 men yelling. Then they started stomping and yelling. The Pier was vibrating. The men from New York were freaking out, they were definitely outnumbered. I guess that guy shouldn't have pulled the string on the girls bikini. All the bouncers came running. they were trying to escort the gentlemen who were causing trouble off the Pier. Here comes Olaf. He goes nose to nose with one of those New York boys in the entryway. I thought they were going to fight. They both acted like racists. Olaf the white. New York man black. It was interesting to watch and I was hoping nobody got hurt. I stood back a little way and watched one of the New York guys reach into his pocket (seemed like for a gun or knife) and he kept saying, "I hate when this happens, I hate when this happens". So I approached Olaf and the other man. I told the other man "we can go to another bar, bring your friends". I was just trying to help calm the drama and not have a riot. Still nose to nose growling at each other, throwing their racist comments back and forth. Male testosterone rampaging. Olaf respected me and backed up. Everyone was being stupid bastards. But they were leaving. I kept saying, "lets go to another bar". They started leaving, and not quietly I must add. The owner of the Pier was watching. Here comes one skinney little summer cop walking towards us. He was trying to be nice and not upset all the people and families visiting the pier and beach. We escorted the trouble makers off the Pier to 4 waiting cruisers. Come to find out they were thrown out of 2 other bars down the beach.

So here I was 5 years later sitting next to Olaf. He was drunk but coherent. I asked him where he got that scar on his eyebrow. Here comes the story. So I bought him a beer. Heineken of course. He was working as a bouncer at the end of the Pier. One night a bunch of Sky Men (motorcycle group) were very unruly and he had to make 6 of them leave. He was the only bouncer that night. They were being disrespectful to the Angels motorcycle group. So here was Olaf in the middle of this drama. Well, Olaf was making the Sky Men leave the Pier. They made it to the end of the Pier and 6 of them jumped him. So here was Olaf fighting with 6 men and he was doing a pretty good job holding his own. When out of nowhere, one of the bikers woman smashes a beer bottle on his head. "See this, he says", as he looms over me. Olaf said he was outnumbered and the Angels saved him. He said he has Angels that love him and keep an eye on him. He meant the Angels motorcycle club. I said I had Angels that keep an eye on me too, but they are Gods Angels and they have really big wings. I told Olaf that if you are a good boy God will protect you too. I feel I have a couple big Angels who protect me, really Olaf. He laughed and went to the men's room. He came back and snuck up behind me (to tease me , but he's strong as an ox and doesn't know his own strength). He kidney slapped me with two hands while I was sitting on my stool. Gee that hurt! I turned towards him as he was lifting his leg to sit on his chair. "That really hurt", I said. Even though he was playing. It was like a cat playing with a pit bull. Facing him I quickly placed my ten fingers on his chest and gave a push to let him know to back up from me. You hurt me you bastard! Next thing I know, he falls backwards 15 feet. Took his chair with him too. Looking up at me, still holding his chair. Laying sideways on the floor, with a shocked look on his face, tangled in his chair. It took him a minute to comprehend the situation he was in. I tipped over Olaf! I hardly pushed him. He deserved it though. He was not hurt. His pride was. He was drunk and off balance. I told him I had Angels with big wings. Love those flight feathers. Two girls who were sitting behind me saw the whole thing, cheered and clapped. I was backing up. He got up . Dusted his big self off (all 350 pounds). He picked his chair up and started to walk towards me with a look in his eye. I ran. I ran into the girls room and locked the door. Not knowing if he is going to kick the door in. In the past I have lifted weights in the gym with Olaf. I was not going to deal with his drunk bull like strength at my 125 pounds. I was not in his weight class. I don't mind playing rough with my men friends, but not when they are drunk and triple my weight. I am not that stupid.

A few minutes later I came out of the girls room. Gave Olaf time to lick his wounded pride. Fucking Viking. Walking out I could see Olaf sitting in his chair at the corner of the bar drinking his Heineken. The room was quiet. Gee, he was a big boy. I walked towards him and set down next to him. Not knowing what to expect. Everyone was watching. He turned to me, eyebrows down, even the one with the scar. "You think you are tough, don't you?", he says. I really hurt his pride. Nobody tips Olaf over. I said, "I told you I had big Angels, bigger than yours". He didn't know what to say to that. He bought me a drink and said, "I want you on my side".

You never know what to expect when you stop in somewhere for a hot chocolate in Maine. It was a good night. Nice crisp Maine air. I left soon after. Had to go finish plowing driveways. Olaf said not to tell people I tipped him over. It is not good for his ego.

SAVING BROOKE BENTLEY

My tenant Brooke Bentley (she has a movie star name) called me. She was having trouble with her kitchen faucet leaking. Can you come over and fix it? Sure I'll be right over to check it out. She said she didn't feel very well so just walk in and take a look. I knocked and walked in, she was laying on the couch. She never lays down. She is a type A personality, always on the go. She is the only other person I have met in my life who talks more than me. I wasn't used to seeing her in this condition. Brooke not talk, she must be sick.

I was puttering around the sink area, looking for the leak. I had to call the plumber. While on the phone with Bob the plumber, I could see Brooke wasn't well. Her son Lorenzo was playing around her while, she lay on the couch. He loves his mom. He was trying to take care of her. This was so cute to watch. Then

Brooke proceeded to stand up and walk into the wall. Something was definitely wrong with Brooke. I had known her for about 10 years and never saw her like this, and her apartment was a total mess, or disaster area was more like it.

Brooke, I said, You have to go to the doctor. Ya, she said. She usually has a lot to say, but she didn't say much, which was very unusual for her. She had a very bad headache she kept saying. We gathered up Lorenzo, locked the door and walked out of her apartment. We will fix the sink later, it ain't leakin on anyone's head right now. Brooke had trouble walking straight. The hospital was only a mile away. We got into my car and went directly to Goodall Hospital. She went in and they admitted her. The staff did a scan on her head and immediately rushed her to Maine Medical Center. She had a mass on her brain, directly on top of the brain stem, but she was coherent.

Poor Brooky. But Lorenzo got to ride in the front of the ambulance to Portland. He ran the lights and siren. If the lights and siren sounded different than usual..that was Lorenzo. Make way for his sick momma. Brooke tried to protect him from the drama, she didn't know what was wrong with her. They arrived at Portland hospital, it was only a half hour drive.

They did more scans on Brooke's brain. It looked like a tumor that was pressing down on her brain stem. If they did not do emergency surgery she might not make it another day. Thank God for good surgeons.

Brooke Bentley is a beautiful young mother and her life continued because of the professional care she received. She had a scar on the back of her head, from the top, down to the middle of her neck. She had staples running down the back of her head.

When I saw her in the hospital, she was coming out of the anesthesia. She was trying to describe what her condition was. She was talking a lot which was good. I told her we would talk later. Later came...the diagnosis of her condition was: When she was a baby in her mothers womb, she was the other part of a twin. Brooke's body absorbed the other twin. In this case, her brain. The other twin did not start to grow until Brooke was 26 years old. That was what her brain tumor was. I always told her it was her evil twin trying to kill her.

This is a very rare condition, and the medical term used to describe this is a paragraph long. I mentioned this condition to a friend Marilyn who usto work for a couple of doctors. She said she knew a 26 year old girl who had the same thing happen to her at that age. I had never heard of peoples bodies absorbing the other twin in the womb.

Well anyway, at least Brooky is alive and Lorenzo has his mom. We love Brooky

TORY SHOT TWO YOUNG MEN

It was about 1 a.m. The phone rang. I was sleepin. The thought crosses my mind, with a call at this time in the morning, I wonder. Drama on Elm Street? Is it one of my tenants? What is wrong now? Or at 1 a.m. summertime...What did they do now?

Logan (one of my tenants) called me. He said he was laying in his bed and he heard what sounded like someone tapping on the front glass window of his apartment, with their fingernails. He had to check it out. It almost sounded like gunfire, he said.

He opened his front door, that opened to the street. He could see clearly in the glow of the street light the local crazy guy Tory (he always wore that funky hat, thats how he knew it was him, even at 500 feet, under the street lights. Tory was walking across the street, arm outstretched with a gun in his hand. Walking directly towards a young man who was standing there. BANG. He shot him. And he shot him again when he was on the ground.

I couldn't believe what I was seeing, said Logan. Tory just shot two guys and walked back into his house. I jumped into my car and sped over to where the guy was hurt. I parked my car to block Tory's line of fire from his house towards me. There were people standing around and more gathering. I called the cops. I got out of my car and stood over the dying guy. He was shot in his belly and heart. There was alot of his friends around crying and screaming. They were holding his hands. I look across the street and there is another young man laying in the ground, not moving. He shot him too, that must have been the first two shots I heard.

One Biddefrog cop showed up, he opened his car door and looked over at us. I yelled to him that all these people just witnessed Tory shoot these two guys. The cop looked at me, got back into his car and drove off. He seemed scared.

The dying men were squirming in the street. Shot, bleeding all over the sidewalk and someone's driveway.

You could tell they didn't want to die. They didn't expect this at all, it showed on their faces.

While Logan was on the phone with me, one of the young men died and the other was on his way. Died at his feet. He couldn't believe it. The cop drove off. Nobody around him had a gun in case Tory came back out on another shooting spree. Logan was parked in the middle of the street, talking with all the young people about what just happened. People were on their knees by the men, crying and praying.

Everyone was waiting for the cops to come back. And why was the ambulance so slow? The fire department was only 1/2 a mile away. It was going on ten minutes since the call was made to 911. Two men shot by Tory. It seemed the cops were scared. The second shooting victim probably would have lived if the ambulance would have gotten there quicker.

There is some history with Tory and the city of Biddefrog, Maine. He sued the city on numerous occasions. He acquired his home (on the same street he shot the men) by playing the reverse racism card. He loved to stalk and harass people. He always said around town that Biddefrog police were afraid of him.

He would come around my buildings (the tenants

would tell me) and say "I own this building, I own this town, and there is nothing the cops can do." I always wondered what he had on them. He creeped me out. When he would come around my buildings the tenants would ask him to leave.

I could always tell when he was around my buildings because he would tear a Dunkin Donuts cup (he always drank hot chocolate) in a spiral shape and throw it on the ground. How many times I walked around my property and found those torn cups from Tory. His trademark. He just shot two people and he has been on my property uninvited. This realization just struck me. Makes my skin crawl to think how many times he was lurking in the dark.

He used to stalk me too. He would go to Biddefrog court and look for victims.

Sometimes I would be in court for evictions and I would see him bee-lining straight for me, to try to talk to me. I always looked for a way to get away from him by walking on the other side of the court house hallway or by dashing into the ladies room quick. I didn't want to talk to him at all. He creeps me out. Tory, super creepy guy. He gets an A+ at that. I even called the Maine State Police, Troop A homicide a year or two before he shot the two guys. I mentioned to the Trooper that we got another weirdo on the prowl over here in Biddefrog, Maine.

On of my tenants, Cindy told me that Tory invited her over to his house (FORT TORY, it said above the door). She said they smoked a joint (marijuana cigarette). She said it tasted really bitter, so she asked for a drink. He gave her some koolaid, and that tasted funny too. She didn't remember what happened next, but she said she woke up naked in his bed with him standing over her. She was scared to death. She knew with Tory's reputation she wouldn't make it out the door alive. Cindy knew he drugged and raped her as she looked up at him hovering over her.

She felt like an actress and just pretended that her clothes fell off, and here she was lying naked in his bed. She was afraid if she threw a fit about laying there naked she wouldn't see her son again. He would probably kill me she thought. Oh I'm sorry Tory, my clothes must have fallen off...sorry. I have to go home to take care of my kid. I gotta go. She made it out the door. She never got dressed so fast in all her life, she said. She was still buttoning her shirt as she was going out the door. She couldn't believe what just happened. She said she went to Biddefrog police department and they did nothing. They didn't even talk to him about the incident. What does Tory have on them? She wondered. We all wonder.

The ambulance finally came. Not a Biddefrog ambulance, but from the next town three miles away. A large crowd had gathered. Everyone was crying. The cops from another town showed up and then the local cops finally came with the swat team. There are alot of apartment buildings in the area so it wasn't long before hundreds of people were in the street. Mostly young people. Everyone was upset. Some people were yelling over to Tory's house a lot of obscenities.

Everyone around knew these two young men who were shot. They were very loved by all their friends. They had a little gang going. Their friends were like their family on this street. A lot of young people around have troubled lives and their friends are closer than their families.

By the time 3 a.m. rolled around there was about a thousand people in the street. The street was blocked off with yellow tape. 100 cops were in the street. Tory would not come out. The cops were calling him on speaker phone and his house phone. He finally answered his phone about 5 a.m. and didn't want to come out. He was afraid someone was going to shoot him. Wasn't he the one who just shot two unarmed men? And he is afraid he is going to be shot?

We could see snipers on a couple roofs across from

Tory's house. There must be 30 police departments covering this. All the local news channels were set up. He still wouldn't come out. Shortly after, he let out of his house a beautiful little 5 year old blonde girl. What was she doing in there? His building was shut down by codes and was uninhabitable because of so many safety violations. People couldn't live there, not even Tory legally. The little girl he sent out had a mom who looked just like her. The mom was not there. I wonder where she was? Maybe down along the highway in Rhode Island.

Tory finally surrendered at 6 am. The crowd was yelling and screaming at him. He had been intimidating a lot of people in the area since he moved in. Well, now he was moving out and going to jail forever.

MY PARTIAL RIDE
HOME 1969

MY HITCHIKING ESCAPADES

I was standing outside the front door of the Commodore
Dance Hall in Lowell, Massachusetts. Aerosmith just
finished playing there. It was about 1 am. It had just
closed. About 30 young people were hanging around
by the front door. I was one of them, though younger
than most, at 13 years old. I was innocent but loved
music at a young age. I grew up listening to the Beatles,
Rolling Stones and Aerosmith. I loved Aerosmith, they
were an up and coming band in 1969, and all the locals
packed the Commodore. That was the place to go in the
day. It was a really good night. But it was all over, time
to go home. We were all hanging around by the front
door, savoring the evening, singing songs to the night.

There was a whole herd of us young people, smoking cigarettes, talking.

I was looking for a ride home, so I put the word out while we were hanging around. Well, this short little creepy guy (gave me a creepy feeling) kept coming up to me to offer me a ride home. I had an uneasy feeling about him, so I kept telling him NO NO NO. I ended up waving goodbye to my friends and headed for the road to hitchhike home. But he must have been listening closely when we were talking cause he knew which way I was hitchhiking home. (That was the way to get around in those days) No sooner had I stopped, turned around, and stuck my thumb out...here comes Mr. Creepy guy ...in his big old gold Chevy two door. I will never forget that car or how far back the door locks were from the front seat. You cant reach them they are so far back.

I needed a ride home I thought as he pulled up. Even though I was nervous. I got into the car. I cant believe I did. But I did. I needed a ride. Now when I have that creepy feeling inside myself about a person or situation I'm in, I listen closer. We ended up talking about the band Aerosmith as he was driving along and my tensions eased. I told him I was going to Chelmsford. Being young and trusting, I agreed to go to the local sand pit and see who was hanging around there and take a smoke break. Yes I was a virgin in case you were wondering. We were chatting about life and he kept asking me out. Again I say NO NO NO. I want to go home. Take me home.

Well next thing you know...he jumped on top of me, held a knife to my side and said "don't move". God...just then I remembered (what a time to remember this) people say in traumatic situations your life flashes before your eyes, or something like that...I could hear the guidance counselor from school say "no matter what happens we always love you". Am I dreaming? Is this a Steven King movie (now I think that) Is this guy really holding a knife to my side while he is trying to tear my clothes off?...while he is chewing on my chin. I was stiff as a board. I was really just a child. I cant believe he is doing this to me. I was in shock. I was scared speechless. I just kept repeating myself to him. Begging please just take me home..take me home, as he kept biting my chin. I was so stiff and held my arms tight in front of me to keep him away from undoing my clothes. I kept fighting him off. I tried to reach that door lock that was so far back. Why do they make door locks that far back? Thank God he wasn't a very big guy. He was about my size. I was 120 lbs at 13 years old. I think the night would have been different if he was stronger.

Well, he could see he was getting nowhere. He seemed to have given up on his attack towards me. He moved back over to the driver seat. I sounded like a broken record, "please just take me home, just take me home." I cried all my black eye makeup off. I musta looked like a raccoon. He got quiet and then started the car and went to drive down the road. I was wiping my eyes. We came to a crossroads in the sand pit and instead of taking a right to leave the sand pit to go to the main road. He took a left, that went deeper into the sand pit.

My heart froze...I was like a deer caught in the headlights of a car. Freeked out...Thinking of what just happened, it looked like it was going to get worse. I said to him "You are going the wrong way", he said "I know". Did he just say that? Alert, alert...red lights flashing in my head. Not a dream. I was in shock. So, fast as lightning I turned around to unlock the car door. That lock was so far back and so hard to reach. He slammed on his brakes. I jumped out and tumbled onto the ground. He clamored out the car after me and dropped his knife on the floor of the car, I could see it glimmer from the glow of the dash board lite. As I was trying to get up off the ground he caught me by my fur cape and spun me around. I tried to scream but nothing came out. I cant believe at a time like this my scream is stuck in my throat. He punched me in my left eye. I saw a million stars exploding. He almost knocked me out. I fell down on my knees in the sand. He was trying to drag me behind a sand dune. I'm thinking..Am I gonna die like this? He was on his knees in front of me trying to tear my clothes off.

Inside of my head something clicked...I said to myself "this guy is gonna kill me, I gotta do something." So I pretended I was going to let him have his way with me, or sex, God I was a virgin. While pretending, I was planning in my mind to fight for my life. But I had to get this stupid fur cape off that I had made. It tied around my neck and it was keeping me from fighting for my life.

I said to him "let me take this cape off" I had my fingers under the leather neck chord of it, and he was trying to choke me with it at the same time I was trying to take it off. Im glad I had my fingers under that chord. I was pretending to be helpful and took it off. He was still trying to choke me with it but I got it untied. Thank God. Now I was ready to fight. I was tough for a skinny 13 year old girl. I grew up on a farm with horses. I looked him right in the face as my cape dropped to the ground. Not a sexy look either. He was my height. I grabbed him and threw him face down on the sand. (Theres that adreneline rush they tell you about that surfaces in you during crisis...I cant believe I was doing this). I jumped on his back and took both of my hands and dug my fingernails into both of his eyes, while he was face down in the sand. I broke all my nails off digging into his eyes. Try to rape and kill me you bastard.

Well, being young and stupid. After I almost dug his eyes out, I tried to be his friend and forgive him and talk about God. God will forgive you I said. I wont tell anyone. Just give me a ride home. Well, he got into his car and he picked his knife up off the floor and put it in his pocket. I got into the car too...slowly. His face was pretty bloody, it was dripping on his pants, he was wiping his eyes. I almost felt sorry for him after what he did to me. But I was alive.

He started the car, backed it up and drove out of the sandpit. The right way out this time. He wanted to know where I lived, to take me home. He was very insistent. He wanted to go on the highway to take me home but I didn't want to go on the highway. They found a dead naked girl on that highway last week. I definitely didn't want to go on Highway 83. I didn't want him to know where I lived. But here I was, in his car, going down the road with a man that just tried to rape and kill me. I was ready to jump out of that car in an instant once we were closer to the city.

We got close to a Dunkin Donuts. I always hated the color pink but at that moment the pink sign was my best friend. Civilization. My friend lived next door. We were ½ a mile from the Commodore, from where our evening began. I told him to drop me off here. I had to be very insistent. I thought I was going to have to fight again. He pulled up to the curb. I jumped out fast. He was still asking where I lived as I exited the car. I looked at his bloody, gouged up face. His eyes were hardly open. I ran for my life.. I had trouble seeing as my left eye was swollen shut. Believe me, I would find my way.

I went to my friend Ronnie's house. I banged on the front door yelling.. "Ronnie, Ronnie...a guy just tried to rape and kill me!" "No he did not he yelled back through the closed door, get out of here I heard you were a runaway." What a time to deal with a friend not opening the door. After almost being raped and killed... and he is worried if I am a runaway? He didn't come to the door. I felt the creepy guy might come back. I hid in the hallway for a while. I looked out and walked over to the closed Dunkin Donuts that had a pay phone outside. I reached into my pouch (I'm surprised I didn't loose that in the struggle, but it was tied to my belt). I found 10 cents. That's all I had to my name and that's what a call costs back then. I was hiding in the bushes afraid the creepy guy would come back. I was trying to decide who to call for a ride to help me. My mom would kill me if she knew I was hitchhiking. So I called my girlfriend Pam's mom.

Sitting there in the corner, hiding in the bushes, I felt like a hunted animal. My left eye was so swollen I couldn't even open it, I was shaking like a leaf. Crouched in the corner like a wounded animal, while I was trying to decide who to call with that thin dime.

A taxi driver pulled up and asked if I needed a ride. He must have seen me hiding there. Too, after what I just went through with a man alone...I was all set for a ride. I wasn't getting into his car. I told him I had a ride. He drove off. I don't think I ever dialed a telephone number so fast as when I was dialing Pam's home number that night. I couldn't tell my mom. Pam answered the phone. I said a guy just tried to rape and kill me, please come get me. I was lucky to be alive. Within 15 minutes Pam's mom pulled up in her old maroon wagon. I jumped in. I didn't look very good. It felt good to be safe. She drove to her house. I just went upstairs and fell asleep. I was exhausted from that experience. Guess what? She called my mother the next morning. I got yelled at.

DRIVING TO WORK ON ROUTE #111

Gorgeous day, driving to work on route #111. Thinking about the jobs to do in an apartment I was working on. I come over a small hill and I look to my left, and there are about 5 white sheriff cars on the opposite side of the road parked. They had some poor sucker in a white truck pulled over. Poor guy, he really must have done something wrong to have that many cruisers pull him over.

Well, Im just passing by this scene, on my way to work. I glance closer at the vehicles and I see it is my son who has been made the poor sucker in his white truck. His friend Euge standing on the side surrounded by cops. Stupid bastards, drama unfolding. Come to find out after, I missed the worst of it. Nice thing a mom has to see on her way to work. As I was passing by, glancing over, I could see my son Logan in the front cruiser, front passenger seat of an unmarked white cruiser. His face looked red like his blood pressure was up. Im thinking to myself "what in hell?"

I don't pass by more than a hundred feet or so and mother grizzly bear syndrome kicks in. I pull a u-turn. This is great I'm thinking, this is all I need. I'm doin this at 50 years old. I gotta turn around and check this out. Gotta go intimidate the cops cause they got my kid. Wonder what he did. Wouldn't you?

Here I come...The Mom. They got my kid those bastards. I'm on a mission. There is some strong force (mother grizzly bear syndrome I call it) that engulfs us mom persons when the children are in need. Even old children. Who might have been stupid bastards. They can see me coming. Saw me took that u-turn in the middle of route #111. Here she comes, the mom person. Oh no, its Fury.

I pulled up to the first group of cops who were surrounding Euge (my sons friend from childhood). I rolled my passenger window down and yelled out "what did you do now Euge?" He just looked at me. They all just looked at me. Flashback to Euge driving his truck drunk last year, when they stopped him, he told them his dog was driving.

I drove a few more feet towards the front cruiser and saw my son get out of the front passenger side. You ok? I yelled. He said yes. At this time I'm blocking the road and cars are building up in a line behind me. Im movin, Im movin...I had to move along. I was freaked out though. Thinkin, what in hell just happened?

Logan goes to his truck and Euge does too. They are being let go. I called my son on the cell. What in hell was that all about? He said "Mom you missed the best part. They had me face down on #111 with guns drawn on me, about 20 cops. They had the traffic stopped in both directions. I didn't even know why until I got into the front cruiser and the cop said someone robbed a Bank in Biddefrog. They saw my truck drive by the bank fast after and thought it was me that robbed the bank. (He lives up the street). They said the guy that did it looked kinda like me. He printed out a picture of the guy in the cruiser and the cop could see it wasn't me.

About that time I see you comin down the road. I said to the detective "here comes my mom." Mom, it was so funny, he actually seemed nervous when I said that. Does he know about mother grizzly bear syndrome? So we got out of the car. I couldn't believe you drove by at that time. I'm glad you didn't come by two minutes earlier when they all had their guns drawn on me and had me lay down in the middle of the road. You wouldn't want to see that. No I wouldn't, I said.

SQUARE POND

I was walking across the porch overlooking Square Pond
, carrying a big kettle of corn on the cob. We were ready
to set at the table to eat a nice lunch on a beautiful day.
Family around. Maine, "the way life should be" grilling,
cookout, the lake...children playing in the sand. The
girls were tanning on the beach. The guys were up in
the garage.

Heading for the table, I heard the girls scream "he cant
swim!" I look over to the pier and see a man jump from
the end of the pier into 10 feet of water. And he couldn't
swim? Splash, splash, splash and he went under. Well,
it was obvious he couldn't swim. He was floundering.
Why does he jump in 10 feet of water if he cant swim?
He was under the water now. Does two seconds really
pass that fast?

The men were up the hill in the garage, doin the guy thing, like guys do in garages.. They couldn't hear the scream because the garage door was facing the opposite direction from the pond. The girls couldn't save him. They were running around screaming in their colored bikinis. The children were frozen in their spots, staring. But there was no splashing now. He went under. All you could see was little ripples in the water. His lungs were not equipped for that environment.

Oh God. Why me?...as I set the kettle of corn down on the porch floor. I think my reaction time was about two seconds. I couldn't believe what I was doing (at 45 years old). Running down the hill to jump off the dock to save this guy, who, I didn't even know his name.

OK, here I go...So here I was running down the hill, the wind blowing my hair back. Kicking off my sandals in the mad rush, getting closer to the end of the pier to dive off. Running the distance of about 200 feet. I had one problem, my glasses. I had my glasses on while in life saving mode. I need my glasses. There are many people out there like me who need their glasses. I would still save the idiot who couldn't swim and jumped into 10 feet of water. But I gotta have my glasses! So I placed my glasses at the end of the pier and dove in. The water was a perfect temperature. If you had to chose a water temperature to save someone's life in, this was it.

I dove exactly to where he was, he was almost standing on the sandy bottom. The water was clear and I could see him trying to swim. His arms were flailing, he was trying to do something, but it wasn't helping him at all to swim. He was sinking like a rock. He looked relieved to see me and was very cooperative. I think to myself, "How do I get sucked into this shit?" As I approached him I could see he was a big guy, about 200 pounds, compared to my 125. I moved quick, there was no time to waste. I reached my left arm under his left arm and across his chest, I pushed off the sandy bottom. Try saving someone's life underwater who is 75 pounds heavier and doesnt even know how to kick his feet to stay afloat.

Thank God we weren't very far off from the end of the pier. This guy was heavy and I had no floatie. When we broke through the surface of the water a young man Daniel (who is now an EMT for a local ambulance) was there at the end of the pier in the water. God this guy was heavy. So I let go of him, dropped under and behind him in the water and pushed him as hard as I could. He was dragging me under. So I pushed his fat ass towards the pier. Daniel was reaching for him, and finally grabbed him. We did it!

Can you believe in the middle of this I glanced up at the pier for my glasses? Everyone came running to help now. The men came down the hill asking "What do you girls want?" They didn't know their friend had almost drowned. We could hear the ambulance coming.

ABOUT THE AUTHOR

Deborah lives in Maine for over 40 years and has been sharing her stories for years. She would stop during the day and tell a story here and there to people. Everyone always said told her she should write a book. Deborah is straight to the point person and as a landlord and her tenants are like family to her. She built her business from nothing and now can share her experiences with readers everywhere.